D0340881

Other books by Exley:
Country Notebook
Flower Arranging Address Book
Flower Lover's Birthday Book
Garden Lover's Book of Days
Garden Lover's Quotations

Published simultaneously in 1992 by Exley Publications in Great Britain, and Exley Giftbooks in the USA.
Reprinted 1992. Third and fourth printings 1993.

ISBN 1-85015-329-9
A copy of the CIP data is available from the British Library on request.
Edited by Helen Exley; Designed by Pinpoint Design
Printed in Hungary.
Exley Publications Ltd, 16 Chalk Hill, Watford, Herts WD1 4BN, U.K.
Exley Giftbooks, 359 East Main Street, Suite 3D, Mount Kisco, NY 10549, USA.
Credits: Archiv Fur Kunst, cover; Bridgeman Art Library; Gavin Graham Gallery, London; ©Curt Herrrmann 1903, Pages: 10, 51; Kunsthistoriche Museum, Vienna, Page 61; Metropolitan Museum of Art, New York, Page 57; Musee d'Orsay, Paris, Pages 20, 37; National Gallery of Art, Washington DC, Page 16; Oldham Art Gallery, Lancashire, Page 33; Tate Gallery London, Page 52; By Courtesy of the Board of Trustees of the Victoria & Albert Museum, Page 19; Victoria Art Gallery, Bath, Page 48; Waterhouse and Dodd, Page 14; Christopher Wood Gallery, Pages 8, 38, 63.
The publishers would like to thank the following for permission to reprint copyright material. They would be pleased to hear from any copyright holders not here acknowledged. "Come-Gone" by Walter de la Mare, reprinted by permission of the Literary Trustees of Walter de la Mare and The Society of Authors as their representative; "Loveliest of Trees the Cherry Now" by A. E. Housman from *Collected Poems,* reprinted by permission of the Estate of A. E. Housman and Jonathan Cape as publisher; Extract from "Fidelity", from *The Complete Poems of D. H. Lawrence* by D. H. Lawrence. Copyright ©1964, 1971 by Angelo Ravagli and C. M. Weekly, Executors of the Estate of Frieda Lawrence Ravagli. Used by permission of Viking Penguin, a division of Penguin Books USA Inc.; "Bounty" by Mary Webb from *51 Poems* reprinted by permission of the Estate of Mary Webb and Jonathan Cape as publisher; "Old Fashioned Flowers" from *Four Seasons* by Leonard Clarke, reprinted by permission of Dobson Books Limited.

FLOWERS

A CELEBRATION IN WORDS AND PAINTINGS

SELECTED BY
HELEN EXLEY

EXLEY
MT. KISCO, NEW YORK • WATFORD, UK

TO FLOWERS!

They grow among desolation.
They shroud the scars of war.
They grant a haven to the desolate.
They bring hope to those who are injured or ill.
They comfort the bereaved.
They mark remembrance.
They cheer city yard and suburban garden.
They defy the machine.
They are lights in darkness.
They are the promise of renewal.
They are life.

PAM BROWN, b.1928

We live among marvels...each flower a masterpiece of subtle beauty, form and scent.

MARION GARRETTY, b.1917

The Amen! of Nature is always a flower.

OLIVER WENDELL HOLMES (1809-94)

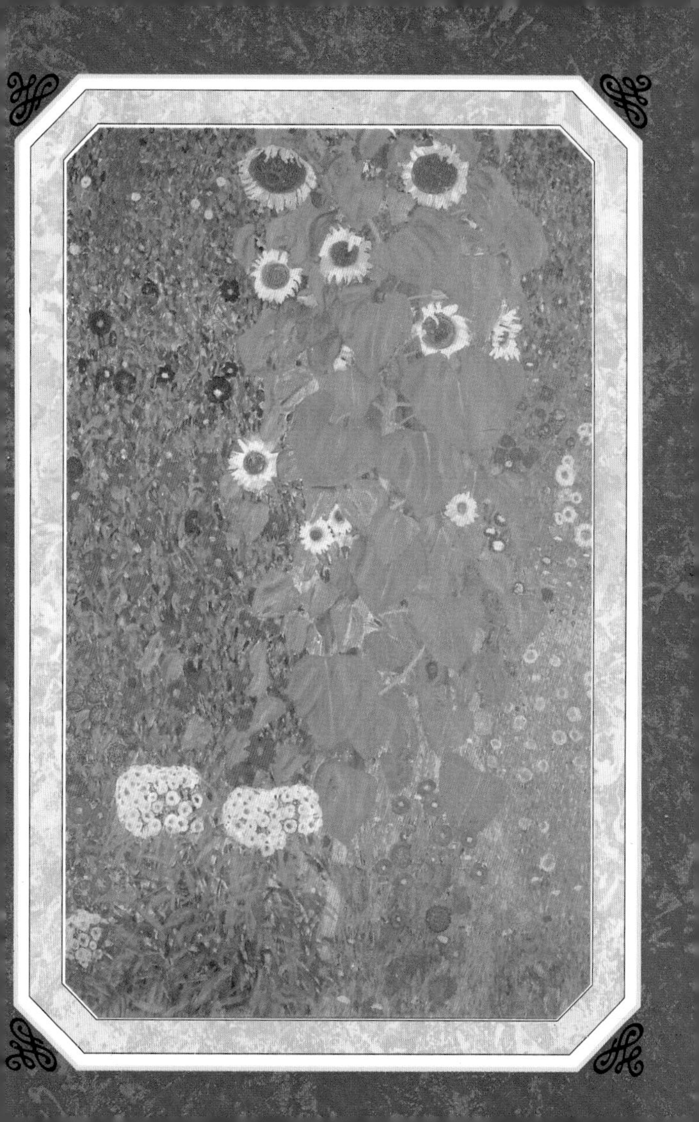

THE SWEETEST THINGS

We are the sweet Flowers
Born of sunny showers,
Think, whene'er you see us, what our beauty saith:
Utterance mute and bright
Of some unknown delight,
We fill the air with pleasure, by our simple breath:
All who see us, love us;
We befit all places;
Unto sorrow we give smiles, and unto graces, graces.

LEIGH HUNT (1784-1859),
FROM *"SONG OF THE FLOWERS"*

Flowers...flowers are the sweetest things God ever made and forgot to put a soul into...

HENRY WARD BEECHER (1813-1887)

NATURE'S JEWELS

See how the flowers, as at parade,
Under their colours stand displayed:
Each regiment in order grows,
That of the tulip, pink and rose.

ANDREW MARVELL (1621-1678)

In emerald tufts, flowers purple, blue,
and white;
Like sapphire, pearl, and rich embroidery.

WILLIAM SHAKESPEARE (1564-1616)

The flowers are nature's jewels,
with whose wealth she decks her summer
beauty.

GEORGE CROLY (1780-1860)

There is no such thing as an ordinary flower.

CHARLOTTE GRAY b.1928

THE MYSTERY OF BEAUTY

Flower in the crannied wall
I pluck you out of the crannies
I hold you here, root and all, in my hand
Little flower - but if I could understand
What you are, root and all, and all in all
I should know what God and man is.

ALFRED, LORD TENNYSON (1809-1892)

We cannot fathom the mystery of a single flower, nor is it intended that we should; but that the pursuit of science should constantly be betrayed by the love of beauty, and accuracy of knowledge by tenderness of emotion.

JOHN RUSKIN (1819-1900)

The scientists know that the colour and patterning of flowers is nothing whatever to do with us - being simply the lure set out for necessary insects. Why then do they shake the human heart?

MAYA PATEL, b.1943

There was never mystery
But 'tis figured in the flowers;
Was never secret history
But birds tell it in the bowers.

RALPH WALDO EMERSON (1803-1882)

PEACE

Flowers...have a mysterious and subtle influence upon the feelings, not unlike some strains of music. They relax the tenseness of the mind. They dissolve its rigor.

HENRY WARD BEECHER (1813-1877)

. . . and it is an agonizing business, to say good-bye to a garden. Often, when the car has been panting outside in the lane, I have run back for one last look . . . there was a lily I had forgotten . . . or a bluebell that was almost blue . . . or a rose that was in hiding, among the quiet shadows on the wall. Desperately I run out, while the car chug-chugs in the distance. The peace of the garden descends upon me. The green leaves enfold me. Time, and the car, they are both forgotten.

BEVERLEY NICHOLS,
FROM *"DOWN THE GARDEN PATH"*

WILDFLOWERS

You gave me dandelions. They took our lawn by
squatters' rights - round suns rising in April,
soft moons blowing away in June.
You gave me lady slippers, bloodroot,
milkweed, trillium whose secret
number the children you gave me tell.
In the hierarchy of flowers, the wild rise on
their stems for naming.
Call them weeds. I pick them as I picked you,
for their fierce, unruly joy.

LINDA PASTAN

Wildflowers are perhaps the most enchanting
of all for me. I love their delicacy,
their disarming innocence, and their defiance
of life itself.

PRINCESS GRACE OF MONACO (1929-1982)

OLD FASHIONED FLOWERS

A garden of old fashioned flowers,
Planted before grandmother was born.
The house was old then, she
Wore bonnets, long frocks,
Sat under cedar trees,
Played with solitaire and rag dolls.
The gillies now along the red wall
Make a gold spring, double daisies are
Little red cartwheels, and primroses with the strange names,
Jack-in-the-green, Hose-in-Hose, Galligaskins, and Clowns,
Speak of damp Ireland, old picture books.
And then in summer, tulips, flaked and striped,
A dream of Holland on a May morning.
And after them, roses, damask and mossed,
Scenting the English air with France and Persia,
Sulphur and shell pink, they keep close company

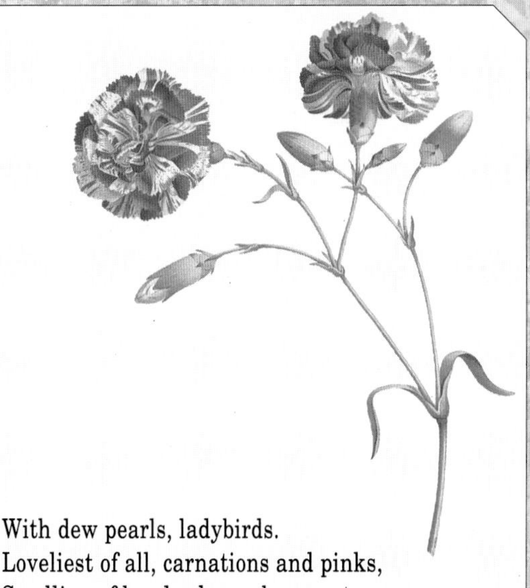

With dew pearls, ladybirds.
Loveliest of all, carnations and pinks,
Smelling of heady clove, sharp nutmeg;
Lining the borders of the smooth lawn,
With mignonette, fragrant verbena.
I make a posy of them all in my mind,
Remember their colours and shapes, when
The garden has only the flowers of the frost,
The smell of dead bonfires.

LEONARD CLARK

The love of flowers kindles rapport across the centuries. Shared enthusiasms, wonder and enquiry render the separation in time irrelevant.

NICOLETTE SCOURSE,
FROM *"THE VICTORIANS AND THEIR FLOWERS"*, 1983

Love of flowers has opened many doors for me. I have made many friends throughout the world because of their love and outstanding knowledge of flowers.

PRINCESS GRACE OF MONACO (1929-1982)

Once we had a great pair of star magnolia bushes flanking the broad brick entrance walk to the front door. While these were in bloom we noticed that none but smiling faces greeted us, so great was the pleasure of mailman, delivery boy, and visitor in the unexpected fragrance that assailed them inside our gate.

HELEN VAN PELT WILSON

Farewell, dear flowers, sweetly your time ye spent . . . I follow straight without complaint or grief, since if my scent be good, I care not, if it be as short as yours.

GEORGE HERBERT (1593-1633)

I love flowers too; not for a young girl's reason,
But because these brief visitors to us
Rise yearly from the neighbourhood of the dead,
To show us how far fairer and more lovely
Their world is; and return thither again,
Like parting friends that beckon us to follow,
And lead the way silent and smiling.
Fair is the season when they come to us,
Unfolding the delights of that existence
Which is below us: 'tis the time of spirits,
Who with the flowers, and, like them,
leave their graves:
But when the earth is sealed, and none dare come
Upwards to cheer us, and man's left alone,
We have cold cutting winter.

THOMAS LOVELL BEDDOES

MEMORIES

Ah, everything has changed since I was a girl, except my flowers; that is why I have them so near me, for they are my oldest friends, so I give them the place of honour.

FROM *"JOURNAL OF HORTICULTURE"*, 1863

Last year, Mrs Miggs was taken out in a car, took tea at the Rectory in the next village, and they stopped here, to give her a sight of the bluebells, and she wept for joy, though her eyes are so dim, now. But she could distinguish the blueness, and smell the flowers, and she said it was exactly the same as she knew it more than eighty years ago.

SUSAN HILL

Siberian wallflowers, night-scented stock,
mignonette. Children's flowers
And in their perfume they hold childhood
safe forever.

PAM BROWN, b.1928

We must learn to look on plants not as mere points of colour, but as old friends on whose coming we can rely, and who, returning with the recurring seasons, bring back with them pleasant memories of past years.

HENRY BRIGHT

A SPRING MORNING

The Spring comes in with all her hues
and smells,
In freshness breathing over hills and dells;
O'er woods where May her gorgeous
drapery flings,
And meads washed fragrant by their laughing
springs.
Fresh are new opened flowers, untouched
and free
From the bold rifling of the amorous bee,
The happy time of singing birds is come,
And Love's lone pilgrimage now finds a home;
Among the mossy oaks now coos the dove,
And the hoarse crow finds softer notes for love.
The foxes play around their dens, and bark
In joy's excess, 'mid woodland shadows dark.
The flowers join lips below; the leaves above;
And every sound that meets the ear is Love.

JOHN CLARE (1793-1864)

THE MIRACLE

Nothing seems to me more surprising than the planting of a seed in the blank earth and the result thereof. Take a Poppy seed, for instance: it lies in your palm, the merest atom of matter, hardly visible, a speck, a pin's point in bulk, but within it is imprisoned a spirit of beauty ineffable, which will break its bonds and emerge from the dark ground and blossom in a splendor so dazzling as to baffle all powers of description.

CELIA THAXTER (1835-1894),
FROM *"AN ISLAND GARDEN"*

All through the winter, beneath forgetful white, these tiny entities remain asleep, recharging their energy until the first thaw of spring. Then, as if touched by magic, within days the mountainsides bloom with patchworks of color. The miracle of nature once more unfolds.

PRINCESS GRACE OF MONACO (1929-1982)

The tight bud cracks.
Out shoulders crumpled silk.
Spreads, smoothes itself.
Shimmers in the sun.
Fades and falls.
All in a day.

So much complexity
to come to this
one moment
of perfection.

But justified.

PAM BROWN, b.1928

Just as if an alarm set within the earth last fall had struck now, they must awake, they must arise, they must live. These plump daffodil buds, even if frozen solid tonight, will not bow in the morning.

BERTHA DAMON

A CONTEMPLATION

Brave flowers, that I could gallant it like you,
And be as little vain;
You come abroad, and make a harmless show,
And to your beds of earth again;
You are not proud, you know your birth,
For your embroidered garments are from earth.

You do obey your months, and times, but I
Would ever have it spring,
My fate would know no winter, never die,
Nor think of such a thing;
Oh, that I could my bed of earth but view,
And smile, and look as cheerfully as you.

Oh, teach me to see death, and not to fear,
But rather to take truce;
How often have I seen you at a bier,
And there look fresh and spruce;
You fragrant flowers then teach me that my breath
Like yours may sweeten and perfume my death.

HENRY KING

Look at the fate of Summer flowers,
Which blow at daybreak,
Droop ere evensong;
And, grieved at their brief date, confess
that ours,
Measured by what we are, and ought to be,
Measured by all that trembling we foresee,
Is not so long.

WILLIAM WORDSWORTH (1770-1850)

SPRING

How many daisies can you count on your lawn?
When you can count twelve daisies,
Spring has come.

ELEANOR FARJEON

Soon o'er their heads blithe April airs
shall sing;
A thousand wild flowers round them
shall unfold;
The green buds glisten in the dews of spring,
And all be vernal rapture as of old.

JOHN KEBLE (1792-1866)

With tumbled hair of swarms of bees,
And flower-robes dancing in the breeze,
With sweet, unsteady lotus-glances,
Intoxicated, Spring advances.

FROM A SANSKRIT POEM

The flowers of late winter and early spring occupy places in our hearts well out of proportion to their size.

GERTRUDE S. WISTER

April in New England is like first love.

GLADYS TABER (1899-1980)

→←

ASK THE APRIL WEATHER

They are all in the lily-bed, cuddled close together -
Purple, yellow-cap, and baby-blue;
How they ever got there you must ask the April weather,
The morning and the evening winds, the sunshine and the dew.

ELLEN M. HUTCHINSON (fl.1880S-1933)

For winter's rains and ruins are over,
And all the season of snows and sins;
The days dividing lover and lover,
The night that loses, the night that wins;
And time remembered is grief forgotten,
And frosts are slain, and flowers begotten,
And in green underwood and cover
Blossom by blossom the spring begins.

ALGERNON CHARLES SWINBURNE (1837-1909),
CHORUS FROM *"ATLANTA"*

...but there...dearer even than nightingales or glow-worms, there is a primrose, the first of the year; a tuft of primroses, springing in yonder sheltered nook, from the mossy roots of an old willow, and living again in the clear bright pool. Oh, how beautiful they are - three fully blown, and two bursting buds! How glad I am I came this way!

MARY RUSSELL MITFORD (1787-1855),
FROM *"OUR VILLAGE"*

I WISH YOU FLOWERS

An astounding bouquet delivered to the door for no apparent reason.
Roses on your birthday:
not in cellophane but in a pot, with a good root-ball and an alluring label
Wild orchids - to be shown only to those sworn to secrecy
Dandelions clutched in a child's hot fist
Primroses under the hedge
White violets
A sudden firework of clear scarlet on a dowdy cactus
A sheet of snowdrops in a long-deserted garden
Doll's house lilies, microscopic in the downland turf
Wild pansies
Marsh marigolds blazing in a boggy acre
Harebells by the roadside
A champion among champion sunflowers, towering above the children's heads

Astonishments in a corner of the garden,
unplanted and unplanned
A buttercup glowing under a small child's chin
Black violas
Growth and vein and form and scent,
Leaf and bud and flower,
Discovered or nurtured,
Brief, precious,
Unique.
Life returning after winter:
Stars to light you through the darkest day.

PAM BROWN, b.1928

OUR INSPIRATION

Flowers are not flowers unto the poet's eyes,
Their beauty thrills him with an inward sense;
He knows that outward seemings are but lies,
Or, at the most, but earthly shadows, whence
The soul that looks within for truth may guess
The presence of some wondrous heavenliness.

JAMES RUSSELL LOWELL (1819-1891)

If I had but two loaves of bread, I would sell one and buy hyacinths, for they would feed my soul.

THE KORAN

Flowers reflect the human search for meaning. Does not each of us, no matter how our life has gone, ache to have a life as beautiful and true to itself as that of a flower?

PHILIP MOFFITT

Flowers have been the inspiration of poets and writers since time immemorial. Their very names - periwinkle, delphinium, dianthus, briar rose, heliotrope, columbine, and morning glory - spill from the tongue in sweet sounds.
Flowers symbolize the evanescence of human life. They are the omens of love and hope. Of beauty and promise. Even of death.

PRINCESS GRACE OF MONACO (1929-1982)

TEACHING US

When at last I took the time to look into the heart of a flower, it opened up a whole new world...as if a window had been opened to let in the sun.

PRINCESS GRACE OF MONACO (1929-1982)

How cool, how delicate, how intricate a flower.
They teach us gentleness of touch.
They teach us how to see.
They waken the heart.

PAM BROWN, b.1928

To see a World in a Grain of Sand
And a Heaven in a Wild Flower,
Hold Infinity in the palm of your hand
And Eternity in an hour.

WILLIAM BLAKE (1757-1827)

WHEN CALIFORNIA WAS WILD

When California was wild, it was one sweet bee garden throughout its entire length, north and south, and all the way across from the snowy Sierra to the ocean.

Wherever a bee might fly within the bounds of this virgin wilderness - through the Redwood forests, along the banks of the rivers, along the bluffs and headlands fronting the sea, over valley and plain, park and grove, and deep, leafy glen, bee flowers bloomed in lavish abundance. Here they grew more or less apart in special sheets and patches of no great size, there in broad, flowing folds hundreds of miles in length - zones of polleny forests, zones of flowery chaparral, stream tangles of rubus and wild rose, sheets of golden compositæ, beds of violets, beds of mint, beds of bryanthus and clover, and so on, certain species blooming somewhere all the year round.

But of late years plows and sheep have made sad havoc in these glorious pastures, destroying tens of thousands of the flowery acres like a fire, and banishing many species of the best honey plants to rocky cliffs and fence corners, while, on the other hand, cultivation thus far has given no adequate compensation, at least in kind; only acres of alfalfa for miles of the richest wild pasture . . . and small, square orchards and orange groves for broad mountain belts of chaparral.

JOHN MUIR (1810-1882),
FROM *"THE WILDERNESS WORLD OF JOHN MUIR"*

LOVELIEST OF TREES, THE CHERRY NOW

Loveliest of trees, the cherry now
Is hung with bloom along the bough,
And stands about the woodland ride
Wearing white for Eastertide.

Now, of my threescore years and ten,
Twenty will not come again,
And take from seventy springs a score,
It only leaves me fifty more.

And since to look at things in bloom
Fifty springs are little room,
About the woodlands I will go
To see the cherry hung with snow.

A. E. HOUSMAN (1859-1936)

The flowers appear on the earth;
the time of the singing of birds is come.

SONG OF SOLOMAN

WINTER VIOLETS

Death-white azaleas watched beside my bed,
And tried to tell me tales of Southern lands;
But they in hothouse air were born and bred,
And they were gathered by a stranger's hands:
They were not sweet, they never have been free,
And all their pallid beauty had no voice for me.

And all I longed for was one common flower
Fed by soft mists and rainy English air,
A flower that knew the woods, the leafless bower
The wet, green moss, the hedges sharp and bare -
A flower that spoke my language, and could tell
Of all the woods and ways my heart remembers well.

Then came your violets - and at once I heard
The sparrows chatter on the dripping eaves,
The full stream's babbling inarticulate word,
The plash of rain on big wet ivy-leaves;
I saw the woods where thick the dead leaves lie,
And smelt the fresh earths' scent - the scent of memory.

The unleafed trees - the lichens green and grey,
The wide sad-coloured meadows, and the brown
Fields that sleep now, and dream of harvest day
Hiding their seeds like hopes in hearts pent down -
A thousand dreams, a thousand memories
Your violets' voices breathed in unheard melodies -

Unheard by all but me. I heard, I blessed
The little English, English-speaking things
For their sweet selves that laid my wish to rest,
For their sweet help that lent my dreaming wings,
And, most of all, for all thoughts of you
Which makes them smell
more sweet than any other
violets do.

EDITH NESBIT
(1858-1924)

FLOWERS WILL FADE

O flowers they fade because they are moving
swiftly; a little torrent of life leaps up to the
summit of the stem, gleams, turns over round
the bend of the parabola of curved flight,
sinks, and is gone, like a comet curving into
the invisible.

O flowers they are all the time travelling
like comets, and they come into our ken
for a day, for two days, and withdraw, slowly
vanish again.

And we, we must take them on the wing,
and let them go.
Embalmed flowers are not flowers, immortelles
are not flowers;
flowers are just a motion, a swift motion, a
coloured gesture;
that is their loveliness. And that is love.

D.H. LAWRENCE (1885-1930)

We destroy the meaning of the wedding bouquet when we settle for silk blossoms. They'll last a lifetime in a bedroom drawer. Fresh flowers will fade - but they were part of life, as we are part of life. They were a living joy and left a living memory. But if our wedding flowers are lost to us too soon - their sisters come to bloom, year after year: renewing hope and love through all the changes that will come.

PAM BROWN, b.1928

SILENT JOY

Thanks to the human heart by which we live,
Thanks to its tenderness, its joys and fears,
To me the meanest flower that blows can give
Thoughts that do often lie too deep for
tears.

WILLIAM WORDSWORTH (1770-1850)

When in these fresh mornings I go into my garden before anyone is awake, I go for the time being into perfect happiness. In this hour divinely fresh and still, the fair face of every flower salutes me with a silent joy that fills me with infinite content; each gives me its color, its grace, its perfume, and enriches me with the consummation of its beauty.

CELIA THAXTER (1835-1894),
FROM *"AN ISLAND GARDEN"*

A SENSE OF PEACE

Arranging a bowl of flowers in the morning can give a sense of quiet in a crowded day - like writing a poem, or saying a prayer.

ANNE MORROW LINDBERG

Be still, my soul. Consider
The flowers and the stars.
Among these sleeping fragrances,
Sleep now your cares.
That which the universe
Lacks room to enclose
Lives in the folded petals
Of this dark rose.

GERALD BULLET (1893-1958)

Where would we be if humanity had never known flowers? If they didn't exist or had always been hidden from our sight...would our character, our morals, our aptitude for beauty, our happiness be the same?

MAURICE MAETERLINCK (1862-1949)

I count my blessings with the flowers, never with the leaves that fall.

LADY BIRD JOHNSON, b.1912

A PASSION FOR FLOWERS

He who is born with a silver spoon in his mouth is generally considered a fortunate person, but his good fortune is small compared to that of the happy mortal who enters this world with a passion for flowers in his soul.

CELIA THAXTER (1835-1894),
FROM *"AN ISLAND GARDEN"*

Everyone loves flowers. They make us happy, they make us smile. And the fact that they arrive without fail each spring, peeking through the dark earth, makes even a hardened pessimist believe in the wisdom of nature. And yet working in the garden on a clear summer day - the air sweet with fragrance, a soft wind rustling through the trees, and the sun shining on all the little masterpieces we call flowers - makes one stop to think how truly fragile all this is.

BARBARA MILO OHRBACH,
FROM *"A BOUQUET OF FLOWERS"*

COME-GONE

Gone the snowdrop - comes the crocus;
With the tulip blows the squill;
Jonquil white as wax between them,
And the nid-nod daffodil.

Peach, plum, cherry, pear and apple,
Rain-sweet lilac on the spray;
Come the dog-rose in the hedges -
Gone's the sweetness of the may.

WALTER DE LA MARE (1873-1956)

There is no monotony in flowers, they are ever unfolding new charms, developing new forms and revealing new features of interest and beauty to those who love them.

JOHN WRIGHT, c.1890,
FROM *"THE FLOWER GROWER'S GUIDE"*

Soon will the high Midsummer pomps come on,
Soon will the musk carnations break and swell,
Soon shall we have gold-dusted snapdragon,
Sweet William with his homely cottage-smell,
And stocks in fragment blow;
Roses that down the alleys shine afar,
And open, jasmine-muffled lattices,
And groups under the dreaming garden-trees,
And the full moon, and the white evening-star.

MATTHEW ARNOLD (1822-1888)

BOUNTY

The full woods overflow
Among the meadow's gold!
A blue-bell wave has rolled,
Where crowded cowslips grow.
The drifting hawthorn snow
Brims over hill and wold.
The full woods overflow
Among the meadow's gold;
The ditches are aglow!
The marshes cannot hold
Their kingcups manifold.
Heav'n's beauty crowds below,
The full woods overflow!

MARY WEBB (1882-1927)

...the earth, gentle and indulgent,
ever subservient to the wants of man,
spreads his walks with flowers,
and his table with plenty ...

PLINY THE ELDER

CHERRY BLOSSOMS

The essence of their beauty
Is that it dies away
So exquisitely quickly.
How could one possibly pay
Even respect to a flower in flower
Day upon day upon day?

YAMABE NO AKAHITO

They flush joyously like a cheek under a lover's kiss;
They bleed cruelly like a dagger-wound in the breast;
They flame up madly of their little hour,
Knowing they must die.

MARY REYNOLDS ALDIS (1872-1949)

Oh, this is the joy of the rose:
That it blows,
And goes.

WILLA CATHER (1873-1947)

The rose cried: "I am generous of largesse
And laughter. Laughingly my petals blow
Across the world; the ribbons of my purse
Snap and its load of coin flies everywhere."

OMAR KHAYYAM

Shed no tear! O shed no tear!
The flowers will bloom another year.
Weep no more! O weep no more!
Young buds sleep in the root's white core.

JOHN KEATS (1795-1821)